AF689108

END PROPERTY TAX NOW

THE CASE FOR TRUE HOME OWNERSHIP IN THE UNITED STATES OF AMERICA

To

From

To every American family who has worked for a home, paid for a home, and sacrificed for a home—believing it should truly be yours: this book is for you.

– **Ryan Chamberlin**
Member, Florida House of Representatives

Access Additional Resources

EndPropertyTaxNow.com/resources

Published by
Kyle Wilson International
KyleWilson.com

Distributed by
EndPropertyTaxNow.com

Cover design by Thomas Griffin
Editing and layout by Takara Sights

End Property Tax Now
ISBN: 978-1-7357428-8-5

Printed in the United States of America

END PROPERTY TAX NOW

THE CASE FOR TRUE HOME OWNERSHIP IN THE UNITED STATES OF AMERICA

RYAN CHAMBERLIN

MEMBER, FLORIDA HOUSE OF REPRESENTATIVES

ENDPROPERTYTAXNOW.COM

The Property Tax Manifesto

We believe property rights are among the most fundamental rights a free people possess.

They are the foundation of independence, security, and opportunity.

We believe government exists to protect property rights—not hold a permanent lien against them.

We believe that property taxes have quietly changed the meaning of ownership. They have turned what should be private property into a perpetual lease, with government as the silent landlord.

Ownership should mean ownership.

Not someday.

Not after another study.

Not after another commission.

Now.

We believe that once you've paid for your home, it should be yours. Completely. Permanently.

This is not about refusing to fund government. It is about funding government without making citizens perpetual tenants on their own property.

Every great reform begins when ordinary citizens refuse to accept that "this is just the way it's always been." This is that moment.

Join us.

Let's make Florida the first state in America where a family can finally say, "This home is truly ours." **Ownership means ownership.**

These are the beliefs that brought me to this fight. The pages that follow are my case for why they matter.

—Ryan Chamberlin
Member, Florida House of Representatives

Disclaimer

The information, opinions, and proposals presented in this book are intended for educational, informational, and public policy discussion purposes only. Nothing contained in this book should be construed as legal, tax, financial, or other professional advice.

The views and opinions expressed in this book are solely those of the author and do not necessarily reflect the official positions, policies, or actions of the Florida House of Representatives or any other governmental entity.

These views are also presented to encourage thoughtful discussion and debate about public policy. References to legislation, constitutional provisions, court decisions, or governmental actions are for informational purposes and should not be relied upon as official legal interpretations.

The discussion of laws, constitutional provisions, and public policy reflects information available at the time of publication and may not reflect subsequent legislative, judicial, or constitutional changes. Readers should consult qualified legal, tax, or financial professionals regarding their specific circumstances before making decisions based on the material in this book.

While every reasonable effort has been made to ensure the accuracy of the information presented at the time of publication, no representation or warranty is made that the information is complete, current, or free of error.

To the fullest extent permitted by applicable law, neither the author nor the publisher shall be liable for any direct, indirect, incidental, consequential, or other damages arising from the use of or reliance upon the information contained in this book.

Buy in Bulk for Discounts and Bonuses

Level	Quantity	Price	Shipping
	1–9	$12.97 ea	Plus Shipping
Basic	10+	$10 ea	FREE SHIPPING plus Bonuses
Bronze	100+	$8.50 ea	FREE SHIPPING plus Bonuses
Silver	250+	$7.50 ea	FREE SHIPPING plus Bonuses
Gold	500+	$6 ea	FREE SHIPPING plus Bonuses
Platinum	1000+	$5 ea	FREE SHIPPING plus Bonuses

FREE SHIPPING for all orders of 10 or more books (US 48 states only)

Basic Sponsorship Bonuses (10+ Books)
Free Shipping plus recognition on EndPropertyTaxNow.com

Bronze Sponsorship Bonuses (100+ Books)
Free Shipping plus Bronze recognition on EndPropertyTaxNow.com
Limited Edition Hardback signed by Ryan Chamberlin
Special Edition Bronze *End Property Tax Now – Challenge Coin*

Silver Sponsorship Bonuses (250+ Books)
Free Shipping plus Silver recognition on EndPropertyTaxNow.com
Limited Edition Hardback signed by Ryan Chamberlin
Special Edition Silver *End Property Tax Now – Challenge Coin*
Ryan will appear for your group on Zoom or by podcast

Gold Sponsorship Bonuses (500+ Books)
Free Shipping plus Gold recognition on EndPropertyTaxNow.com
Two Limited Edition Hardbacks signed by Ryan Chamberlin
Two Special Edition Silver *End Property Tax Now – Challenge Coins*
Ryan will appear on Zoom, a podcast, or **live at your event**

Platinum Sponsorship Bonuses (1000+ Books)
Free Shipping plus Platinum recognition on EndPropertyTaxNow.com
Five Limited Edition Hardbacks signed by Ryan Chamberlin
Five Special Edition Silver *End Property Tax Now – Challenge Coins*
Ryan will appear on Zoom, a podcast, or **live at your event**
Private lunch or dinner with Ryan before your event

To order go to
EndPropertyTaxNow.com/book

Founder Quotes

"We cannot be happy, without being free—that we cannot be free, without being secure in our property—that we cannot be secure in our property, if, without our consent, others may, as by right, take it away."
—John Dickinson, *Letters from a Farmer in Pennsylvania* (1768)

"Now what liberty can there be, where property is taken away without consent?"
—Samuel Adams, "The Rights of the Colonists" (1772)

"No power on earth has a right to take our property from us without our consent."
—John Jay, "Address to the People of Great Britain" (1774)

"The right of property is the guardian of every other right, and to deprive a people of this, is in fact to deprive them of their liberty."
—Arthur Lee, *An Appeal to the Justice and Interests of the People of Great Britain* (1775)

"[The people] cannot be taxed or deprived of their property for public uses without their own consent or that of their representatives so elected."
—George Mason, Virginia Declaration of Rights, Section 6 (1776)

"A just security to property is not afforded by that government, under which unequal taxes oppress one species of property and reward another species."
—James Madison, "Property", National Gazette (1792)

JOIN THE MOVEMENT

The conversation starts with this book.
The movement starts with you.

Whether you're ready to take action today or simply stay informed, everything starts with one scan.

EndPropertyTaxNow.com

Scan to join the movement and:

- Sign the Petition
- Stay Updated
- Volunteer
- Sponsor More Books

Together, we can make Florida the first state where **ownership means ownership.**

Acknowledgements

As an elected official, I often get public credit for work that belongs to many people. A name goes on a bill, a face goes in front of a camera, and it's easy for people to believe that one person moved the mountain. But eliminating property taxes isn't a moment—it's a process. And in that process there are many people who, without them, there would be no progress at all. Any credit that might land on me really belongs to a much larger group.

There is no way I could ever mention all the names I've communicated with, or everyone who has helped move this conversation forward. But I do want to acknowledge a few. And about the names I mention here, I want to be clear: none of them have endorsed this book or any specific plan inside it. What they all have in common is this—every one of them is looking out for the best interest of the people, and every one of them remains involved in the ongoing discussions about how we make things better.

Let me start with a portrait on a wall.

When you're standing in the chamber at the Capitol with the other 120 legislators, you can look up above the roster, all the way around the room, and see the portraits of about 50 of Florida's previous speakers of the Florida House of Representatives. Approximately 10 portraits ago, in recent history, is one of **Marco Rubio**—now our Secretary of State. During his time as speaker of the Florida House, he made a historic push toward a property tax overhaul. It didn't end up the way he wanted it to. But that effort became the starting point for so many of the conversations I've taken on here, 20 years later. He deserves credit for his leadership, and for having the courage to start.

The next names belong to the people who made sure the conversation didn't die in a drawer.

In 2023, once I filed **HB 1371** to eliminate property taxes, the bill was assigned to several committees. That's the normal process before a bill can ever be heard on the House floor—and it's also where most bills quietly disappear. Hundreds of bills each year never get heard at all. The key to ever having your bill voted on begins with getting it approved to be heard in committee in the first place. At that time, the House Chairman of the Ways and Means Committee was **Stan McClain**. Without him, my original bill would never have been heard or debated. And none of that would have been possible without the approval of the then-Speaker of the Florida House, **Paul Renner**, who gave this issue the room it needed to breathe.

A bill in the House is only half of the fight. To carry real weight, it needs a companion in the Senate—and those Senate companion bills brought legitimacy to the entire conversation. My property tax partners on the Senate side began with Senator **Jon Martin**, then Senator **Jay Collins**—now our lieutenant governor—and then Senator **Blaise Ingoglia**, now Florida's chief financial officer. Each of them was willing to put their name next to a big idea before it was safe or popular to do so.

In 2026, I had the privilege of being added to the House Select Committee on Property Taxes. Inside a single session, that committee worked through several bills alongside more than 25 other House members. Among them was Representative **Judson Sapp**, who has been a local ally on anything and everything property tax related, and who has been excited about the movement to eliminate and replace from the very first conversation we ever had about it.

I also want to mention Governor **Ron DeSantis**. Although his term is coming to an end, he has done a great deal over the past year to elevate this conversation and give it the attention it deserves.

The names I've mentioned so far are the elected officials I've worked with directly. But behind them stands a much bigger circle. There are countless local political clubs, county commissioners, property appraisers, sheriffs, school board members, former politicians, and policy experts I continue to engage with as we drive this forward. Many of them will never have a portrait on a wall or a name in a headline. They do the work anyway.

Thank you all for your input, your time, and your willingness to keep having a hard conversation. Now it's time to take what we've learned—and get to work.

Dedication

To Jenny, my wife, who stands beside me and believes in me every step of the way. None of this happens without you.

To our four sons, our daughters-in-law, and our grandson Asher—you are why legacy matters. You are why this fight matters.

And to every American family who has worked for a home, paid for a home, and sacrificed for a home—believing it should truly be yours: this book is for you.

With God's help, we'll leave them something no one can tax away.

"A just security to property is not afforded by that government, under which unequal taxes oppress one species of property and reward another species: where arbitrary taxes invade the domestic sanctuaries of the rich, and excessive taxes grind the faces of the poor..."

—James Madison, "Property," essay published March 29, 1792

Table of Contents

"Property must be secured, or liberty cannot exist."

—John Adams

Introduction

Try a little experiment.

Imagine you stop paying your property taxes. You paid off the mortgage years ago. The deed has your name on it. The bank is gone. By every common-sense definition of the word, the house is yours.

Now wait.

A letter comes. Then another. Then a notice with a date on it. And if you keep ignoring them, one day the government you already paid—for the roads, the schools, the deputies, all of it—will put a lien on your home so that when the time comes for your kids to inherit your most prized asset—it could be sold on the courthouse steps to pay any and all back taxes.

So here's the question this whole book is built around: if someone can require you to pay them every single year for something you bought for as long as you live, who actually owns it?

You don't.

You're renting. You've been renting the entire time. And your landlord is the most expensive one in America—because you also paid to build the house.

That's not freedom. That's a lien on the American dream. And the goal of this book is simple: to compel you to join a plan to abolish and replace the system that did this to us.

We're talking about property taxes. The most hated tax in America. Ask a thousand people across the political spectrum to name a tax they'd kill tomorrow, and this one wins going away.

There are two ways to fix it. One is a legislative plan—bills, committees, the hard grind of the Capitol. The other is a citizen-led ballot process that puts it straight in the hands of the people, where it belongs. That second one requires signatures. Lots of them. More than you think. And that's where you come in.

The pages ahead will make the case.

> *"We are not asking permission. We are exercising it—the way free people in a constitutional republic are supposed to."*

My name is Ryan Chamberlin. I live in Central Florida with Jenny, my wife of 32 years. We have four adult children and one grandchild, and I'm 52 years old—which means we started young, and Jenny would want me to remind you that we haven't slowed down since.

I have lived in Florida for the majority of my life, and so has my wife, whose parents came to Florida from Cuba. What affects Floridians matters to me.

I came to politics the long way. Before any of this, I spent 25 years as an entrepreneur and multiple-business owner—a guy who built things and learned how real money actually moves through a real economy. I'm also an author, an advisor, and as of 2023, a member of the Florida House of Representatives for District 24.

I didn't come to Tallahassee looking for a cause. I came looking for answers. The deeper I dug into Florida's tax system, the more convinced I became that property taxes aren't just unpopular—they're fundamentally incompatible with the idea of true ownership.

Since then, I've spent countless hours talking with economists, local officials, policy experts, business owners, and everyday Floridians about one question: if we eliminate property taxes, what replaces them? This book is the result of those conversations.

So Why Here? Why Now?

Because, in plain terms, this is about a violation of the very principles our founders were willing to die to protect.

John Adams said it as clearly as anyone ever has: "Property must be secured, or liberty cannot exist." He understood something we've let ourselves forget—that you cannot be a free man and a permanent tenant at the same time. The two ideas cancel each other out.

And right now, the government holds a lien on your property. On every property. They shouldn't—period. The system is built on a quiet little lie hiding underneath all the paperwork: that government is the true owner of all land, and the rest of us are just renters who are current on this year's bill.

In November 2028, we get the chance to abolish that.

Because look at what this system has done to us in just the last four years:

- Property taxes in Florida are up more than 50%.
- The average age of a first-time homebuyer has climbed to over 40. A whole generation is being priced out of ever owning a front door of their own.
- We're trending towards the highest foreclosure ratio in Florida's history.
- We are being forced to pay taxes on unrealized gains—taxed on money we haven't made, on the paper value of a home we never sold and never intend to. Think about it—you're paying taxes on your equity.

And all of it for what?

So that local governments can spend every dime they take in—and in too many counties, spend it in the most reckless ways imaginable, with no real accountability for where it goes. Then they turn around and tell the public that if we cut a single expense, the schools will close and the streets won't be safe.

Let me say it plainly so there's no confusion: **this is not the truth**. Nobody—nobody—is talking about defunding the things that actually keep us safe and educate our kids. We're talking about finally paying for them in an honest way.

And this book lays out the plan to do exactly that.

Yes, we have real things to pay for. I've never pretended otherwise. But Florida runs a **$1.8 trillion**

economy. In an economy that size, the idea that the only way to fund a deputy or a fire truck is to put a permanent lien on Grandma's paid-off house is not a fact. It's a failure of imagination—and a convenient one for the people collecting the check.

By the time you finish this book, I hope you will better understand the argument I'm making and what's at stake. And then you can decide if you believe, as I do, that what's happening to Florida homeowners is not just inconvenient—it is wrong. And that we can fix it. You can learn more and sign the petition at **EndPropertyTaxNow.com**.

The dream of owning your home—truly owning it, without a government lien perpetually attached to your front door—is not a radical idea. It's the idea this country was built on.

It's time to reclaim it.

"Nobody—nobody—is talking about defunding the things that actually keep us safe and educate our kids. We're talking about finally paying for them in an honest way."

—Ryan Chamberlin

Part One

The Most Hated Tax in America

I walked to the podium and set my notes on the table.

Calling it nerves would be an understatement. Standing before me were roughly 20 seasoned legislators of the Ways and Means Committee—men and women who had spent years navigating the halls of the Florida House of Representatives. And I was about to present my very first bill as a newly elected official.

The bill was House Bill 1371. The first of its kind in over 20 years. It proposed something that, depending on who you asked, was either long overdue or politically impossible: **the complete elimination of property taxes in the state of Florida.**

This bill was arguably the most ambitious proposal for property tax reform introduced in Florida in more than two decades.

The last person to drive a message like this through the system was former Florida Speaker of the House Marco Rubio. While he made meaningful progress, the effort ultimately fell short. The entrenched interests, the complicated revenue dependencies, and the sheer inertia of a 200-year-old system proved too great.

But I didn't know all of that when I walked up to the podium that day. What I did know—and had campaigned on and come to believe deeply—was that property taxes, and the trajectory they were on, were simply wrong. Not just economically wrong. Not just politically inconvenient. Morally wrong. And if no one else was going to say it plainly, I was.

So I laid out the case. Four reasons why the current property tax system is fundamentally broken and why it deserves not reform, but full replacement.

This book covers all four of those reasons—and then goes further, discussing what a better, fairer system might actually look like.

REASON 1: YOU DON'T OWN IT

These four words are not just a theme or a slogan. They are a legal and practical reality for every property owner in America.

No matter how long you have lived in your home. No matter how many years of mortgage payments you have made. No matter how much sweat, sacrifice, and savings you have poured into your property—you do not own it. Not completely. Not in any meaningful sense of the word. Not in any way our nation's Founders would have recognized.

What you have, at best, is a conditional occupancy arrangement with your local government. You are permitted to live on your land and call it your own—provided you continue to pay an annual fee to the government in perpetuity. Miss that payment, and the government can place a lien on your property. Continue to miss it, and they can seize your home entirely.

"At best, the government requires you to pay rent—indefinitely—on the property you thought you owned."

Think about what that means in practice. You spend 30 years making mortgage payments. You sacrifice vacations, delay retirement, and make financial decisions for three decades with the singular goal of paying off your home. The day finally arrives. The bank releases its claim. You hold the deed. And then—nothing changes. The bill still comes. The government still expects payment. The only difference is the name on the invoice.

At that point, what do you actually own? If failing to make a required payment can ultimately cost you the property, then ownership begins to look a lot like a permanent rental agreement. After you've worked 30 years to write that final mortgage check, the government continues collecting its payment year after year. And when you're gone, your children may inherit the deed, but they inherit the lease as well. The government still expects its payment. We call it ownership, but if your children must continue paying for the privilege of keeping the property, what exactly have they inherited—a piece of land or a perpetual lease?

This is, in effect, an undisclosed second mortgage—one that never ends and one that no one adequately explains to you when you sign the papers on your home. The bank told you exactly when your mortgage would be paid off. No one told you that a different payment would continue until the day you die... and beyond.

If you are unable to pay, the government can seize your property. Not the bank or a private creditor. The government—the same government that taxed the income you used to buy the home. The same government that taxed the materials when it was built. The same government that taxed the closing costs, the recording fees, the transfer of title. After all of that—after the home is "yours"—they still hold a permanent, automatic lien against it. Eventually, when the home you've paid off is inherited by your kids, it can be taken away from your family to pay taxes—simply because you never owned it!

We've seen the headlines. The 87-year-old widow in Minnesota who lost her condo over $15,000 in unpaid taxes—and the county sold it for $40,000 and kept every penny. The Detroit homeowners stripped of equity their families had built over generations.

I have spoken to homeowners across Florida who paid off their homes at 50 or 55 years old, fully expecting financial relief in retirement, only to find themselves locked into a government payment that grows larger every year. For many of them, property taxes have become the single greatest threat to their ability to remain in their home—not crime, not deteriorating infrastructure, not medical bills. Property taxes.

"Somewhere in Florida, a 100-year-old homeowner may own the deed, own the memories, and own the mortgage-free title—but still has to pay the government every year for permission to stay—and has likely been paying this rent for close to 80 years."

This is not a small problem. This is a structural injustice baked into the foundation of how we define property ownership in America.

I want to be direct about where I stand: I do not believe the government should hold a lien on anyone's private property. Not your home. Not your business. Not your investment properties. The right to truly own property—free and clear, without an ongoing government claim against it—is, or should be, a cornerstone of the American promise. We will discuss, in later sections, how the essential services currently funded by property taxes can and should be funded differently. There are better ways.

"The American Dream was never meant to come with a permanent lien."

REASON 2: UNREALIZED GAINS

The second reason the property tax system must be replaced will make you furious once you understand it clearly. Because what we are describing is not a tax policy quirk or an administrative inconvenience. It is a fundamental violation of how taxation is supposed to work in a free society.

We are taxing people on money they have never received.

In the financial world, this is called taxing unrealized gains—charging someone for the increased value of an asset they still own and have not sold. You're paying tax on your equity. On the paper value of an asset you have not sold and may never sell.

In virtually every other context in American life, this concept is considered radical, unconstitutional, and politically toxic. Yet it is exactly what the property tax system does, every single year, to every single property owner in the country.

Let me make this concrete with an analogy.

Imagine one day you received a call from the IRS. The agent on the other end of the line is pleasant enough. He says, "Well, we got your taxes. Looks like you reported $50,000 in income this year. But here at the IRS, we've decided you should have made $150,000. So we want you to pay your income tax on $150,000 instead—including the $100,000 you never actually earned."

There would be riots in the streets. And yet this is precisely what we allow to happen with property taxes—every single year.

"You're paying tax on your estimated equity. On the paper value of an asset you have not sold and may never sell. In virtually every other context in American life, this is unconstitutional."

Here is how it works in practice. You purchase a home for $100,000. Over the next decade, property values in your area rise significantly—perhaps because of a strong local economy, new development, or simply increased demand. Your home is now assessed at $500,000. You have "gained" $400,000 in value.

Except you haven't. Not a single dollar of that gain has ever appeared in your bank account. You have not sold the home. You have not refinanced and extracted equity. You have simply continued living in the same house, on the same street, as you did 10 years ago. But now, the government expects you to pay taxes on $400,000 of wealth that exists only on paper—wealth that evaporates the moment the market shifts, and wealth that you may never realize.

And if you never sell? If you live in that home for the rest of your life? You will pay taxes on that unrealized appreciation until you die. Every year. Without exception. Whether you can afford it or not. Whether your income went up or not. Whether your wages kept pace with inflation or not.

There is one more layer to this that makes it even more frustrating: you do not get to determine what your property is worth. A government employee—a bureaucrat who has likely never set foot in your home—makes that determination. They look at comparable sales in your neighborhood, apply formulas and multipliers, and hand you a number. If you believe the number is wrong, you can appeal. But the burden of proof is largely on you, and the process is deliberately time-consuming and opaque.

To summarize: property taxes charge you annually on wealth you may never actually receive, based on a valuation you did not set, determined by someone who does not know your home, on behalf of a government that can enforce its valuation whether you agree with it or not. And we accept this as normal.

We should not.

REASON 3: A DECEPTIVE MODEL

The third reason the property tax system must be replaced is that it is both complicated and deceptive. Almost nobody understands how it works. Not the people paying it. Not, in many cases, the people administering it.

In the course of building the case for Freedom 1-2-3 a complete elimination and replacement plan we'll go over in the next part of the book, (three bills I filed in 2026), I traveled extensively across the state of

Florida. I met with county commissioners, city council members, property appraisers, tax collectors, real estate attorneys, and veteran realtors. I asked every one of them the same question: can you explain how the current property tax system works—how the money is calculated, how it is collected, and where it goes?

Not one of them could do it.

I am not talking about politicians dodging a difficult question. I am talking about people whose professional lives revolve around property taxes—and even they could not trace the full picture. The reason is not that these individuals are uninformed. The reason is that the system has been designed, whether intentionally or through decades of accumulated complexity, to be impossible to fully understand.

Consider what we are working with. There are 38 major exemptions built into the Florida property tax code, each developed over the past several decades in response to different lobbying efforts, political pressures, and well-intentioned but patchwork reforms. Each county then applies its own formulas—its own interpretations, its own adjustments—to determine what is actually owed. The result is a system so fragmented and inconsistent that two neighboring counties with similar populations and similar needs can produce wildly different tax outcomes for property owners with nearly identical situations.

Again, we have in the current model:

- 38 major exemptions layered on top of one another over the last few decades
- County-by-county formulas that vary so dramatically that two neighbors on the same street in different jurisdictions can pay wildly different bills
- Special districts and assessments that fund line items most voters would never approve at the ballot box
- Carve-outs, caps, portability rules, Save Our Homes adjustments, and just-value vs. assessed-value vs. taxable-value calculations
- And a small army of attorneys, consultants, and software vendors who make a very good living interpreting the maze

If you can't explain it, you can't audit it. If you can't audit it, you can't control it.

> *"A tax system that is too complicated for anyone to fully explain is too complicated for anyone to be held accountable to."*

And then there is the millage rate.

The millage rate is the figure that is multiplied against a property's taxable value to determine the annual tax bill.

Many county governments have made a political habit of announcing that they have "lowered the millage rate"—and technically, they are correct. The rate went down. What they neglect to mention is that the taxable value of properties in their county increased dramatically, so despite the lower rate, the actual dollar amount property owners owe went up significantly.

This is not a rounding error or a communication problem. It is a structural deception embedded in the way the system operates. Governments get to claim fiscal restraint while simultaneously collecting more money. Taxpayers get a press release about lower rates while they write a larger check.

"Lowering the millage rate while property taxes go up is like a store advertising a sale while quietly raising prices."

The numbers in Florida make this undeniable. Between 2022 and 2026, the millage rate was reduced in more than 60 of Florida's 67 counties. That sounds like good news. It wasn't. Over that same period, property taxes increased by an average of 50% statewide. In some counties, the increase exceeded 80%.

How do you reconcile a "millage rate cut" with a 50% to 80% tax increase? You don't. You stop pretending the millage rate matters and you start looking at the bill.

The rate went down. The bill went up. By 50% to 80%. In four years.

Inflation during that period ran between 5% and 10%. Wages grew at a similar pace, if that. But property taxes—the mandatory annual payment that determines whether you can remain in your home—grew at five to eight times the rate of the broader economy. For retirees on fixed incomes, for young families trying to build equity, for small business owners operating on thin margins, this is the difference between stability and crisis.

The system isn't just complicated. It's designed to be confusing, because confused taxpayers are compliant taxpayers. A transparent system would have one rate, one method, one place every dollar goes, and one statement every taxpayer could read in five minutes. A transparent system is exactly what we don't have.

A tax system that cannot be explained, that obscures its own growth, and that bears no relationship to the economic realities of the people paying it is not a system worth reforming. It is a system worth replacing.

REASON 4: FRAUD AND WASTE

The fourth reason the property tax system must be fundamentally overhauled generates considerable noise in the media yet remarkably little action in the legislatures: fraud.

Everyone acknowledges it exists. Few have the institutional will to confront it at the scale required. And in the context of property taxes—where the money flows through a labyrinth of county governments, special districts, and administrative bodies—fraud is a central problem.

I want to be careful here, because not every county is equally affected, and not every administrator is culpable. There are honest, hardworking local officials across this state and this country who manage their budgets responsibly. But the system as designed—opaque, complex, fragmented—creates conditions in which fraud not only can occur, but is extraordinarily difficult to detect and even harder to prosecute.

When money flows without accountability, accountability disappears.

Across the board, the trend has been moving in the wrong direction:

- Less transparency about how dollars are spent
- More off-budget vehicles—special districts, authorities, Community Redevelopment Agencies (CRAs), public-private partnerships—that obscure the trail
- Slower and weaker auditing, with elected oversight stretched thin
- More political pressure to fund pet projects through property tax revenue that voters would reject if asked directly

That's not a recipe for accountability.

It is my belief that in many states, a complete fraud-and-waste overhaul of the existing budget could result in a drastically reduced—or in some cases eliminated—

property tax burden for primary homeowners. Without sacrificing a single police officer, firefighter, or teacher. That is a significant claim, and I make it deliberately.

Here is an example that illustrates what we are talking about. In 2025, the state of Florida collected approximately $65 billion in property taxes. Of that, roughly $18 billion came directly from primary residences—homes protected by the Homestead Exemption. That $18 billion dollars represents money paid by ordinary Florida families to live in the homes they call their own.

Florida's current chief financial officer, Blaise Ingoglia, has undertaken an aggressive effort to audit and reform state spending—what has been informally called a DOGE-style overhaul of state government. The preliminary results have been striking. Billions of dollars in fraudulent or improper expenditures have already been identified. And this does not include the far broader category of wasteful spending—expenditures that may be technically legal, but that the vast majority of Florida taxpayers would never have approved had they been asked.

Let's look again:

- Billions in fraud that should never have been spent
- Billions in waste that nobody can defend with a straight face
- Billions in mission-creep spending funded by property taxes that voters never approved

And remember: we only need to find roughly $18 billion to fully eliminate property taxes on every primary home in Florida.

"It is my belief that cleaning up fraudulent and wasteful spending alone could allow Florida to eliminate property taxes for primary homeowners—without cutting a single dollar from police, fire, or education."

If fraud accounts for even a fraction of what early investigations suggest, and if we layer on top of that the elimination of spending that simply does not reflect the priorities of the people being taxed, we are looking at a fundamentally different fiscal picture—one in which the $18 billion currently taken from Florida homeowners is not a necessity, but a habit.

Habits can be broken. Systems can be rebuilt. But only if we are honest about what the current system actually is.

The Bottom Line

Property taxes across the United States are increasing at a rate that is economically unsustainable and morally indefensible.

The argument made by defenders of the current system is familiar: eliminate or reduce property taxes, and the sky will fall. Schools will close. Fire stations will go dark. Law enforcement will be defunded. Public services will collapse.

This argument is false. And deep down, I believe the people making it know it is false.

What is true is that state and local governments have become accustomed to receiving revenue without accountability. What is true is that the current system allows spending growth that would never survive a direct vote by the people being taxed. What is true is that the answer to "where does the money go?" is, in too many jurisdictions, genuinely unknown—even to those responsible for spending it.

The sky will not fall. But the status quo cannot continue.

The reality is that most states, including Florida, have the resources, the revenue mix, and the political horsepower to fund the things that actually matter—public safety, infrastructure, schools—without holding a permanent lien against every roof in the state. There are fairer ways to collect the revenue we genuinely need. There are smarter ways to prioritize the dollars we already have. And there are honest ways to ask voters what they're willing to fund.

It will fall to the legislature—to elected officials with the spine to take the heat—to design the replacement in a principled, scalable, durable way.

This book is about doing what is right. It is about examining every option on the table—not from a partisan position, but from a principled one. It is about uprooting and replacing a 200-year-old system that has grown far past anything the Founders would have tolerated, and far past anything the Founders would have recognized as American.

And above all, it is about restoring what was supposed to be at the heart of the American dream: the genuine, unconditional right to *own* your home.

Not to rent it from the government. ***To own it.***

Part One

Key Takeaways

You don't truly own your home—it's a conditional occupancy backed by a government lien enforceable for life, even after the mortgage is paid.

You're taxed on money you've never received—rising home value is unrealized, unsold paper wealth, yet it's taxed every year regardless.

You don't set your own valuation—a government assessor does, and the burden of proof in a dispute falls on the homeowner.

The system is deliberately hard to explain—for example, in Florida 38 exemptions and county-by-county formulas confuse even the officials who administer it.

"Lower millage rate" is a shell game—Florida cut rates in 60+ counties (2022–2026) while actual bills rose 50–80%, far outpacing inflation.

Fraud and waste is bigger than you think—audits have already found billions in improper spending— potentially enough to cover most of what is needed to eliminate homeowner property taxes entirely.

The goal is replacement, not reform—essential services can be funded through fairer means, restoring real, unconditional home ownership.

Take the next step.
Visit the website to learn more.

EndPropertyTaxNow.com

Part Two

The Road to Elimination

In May of 2026, Governor Ron DeSantis called a special session of the Florida Legislature. This was no ordinary special session. It was dedicated to a single idea: that the House and Senate would pass his proposal to create the largest homestead property tax reduction in Florida history, building toward a scenario where most homeowners would eventually pay little—or even zero—property tax on their primary home.

For this to become reality, the proposal had to make it onto the November 2026 ballot and then win the approval of 60% or more of Florida voters. Both chambers passed what is known as House Joint Resolution 1 (HJR 1), and that historic idea was set in motion toward the ballot.

Sounds simple, right?

Before I explain why it isn't, let me say this. I've now served under Governor Ron DeSantis for over three years. In my opinion, he was the right man at the right time, and he will go down in Florida history—and in our country's history—as one of the greatest governors of all time. Very few governors would take on a lift this heavy in their final months in office. But if you know Ron DeSantis, you know he is not afraid to push the envelope.

Here's the deal, though.

HJR 1 doesn't eliminate the lien the government holds on your home. It doesn't address other property you own. And it doesn't end the fundamental flaws we walked through in Part 1.

What it does, in addition to creating billions in property tax relief—and this is no small thing—is light a fuse. It forces the conversation. It creates the catalyst that opens the door to the legislation that can take place over the next few years and allow Florida to become the first state in the United States where you don't pay the government rent.

That's the prize. And it's bigger than HJR 1.

What This Book Is Not About

This is not a book about lowering property taxes. It is not a book about capping the rate of increase, expanding homestead exemptions, or trimming the edges of a broken system. This book is about eliminating the fundamental flaws we outlined in Part One—because they're just not right.

"If we could develop a better way—shouldn't we?"

And if they're not right for a homeowner, then in my opinion, they're not right for the small business owner either. They're not right for the family who saved up for a vacation cabin, the farmer holding the land his grandfather worked, or the church that owns the building next door so the youth group has somewhere to meet.

In 2026, the state of Florida will collect over $65 billion in property taxes. Roughly $18 billion of that comes from homestead-exempt properties—the primary homes Governor DeSantis is rightly trying to relieve. But homeowners are only part of the story.

Relieving property taxes on primary homes would still leave roughly $47 billion being collected from Florida's small business owners, vacation property owners, commercial properties, agricultural land, rental homes, and just about every other piece of deeded property in the state.

Now, there is a real and worthy debate to be had about how we handle out-of-state investors and national chains versus the family-owned businesses that have been on Main Street for 30 years. We'll get to that.

But here is the premise of this part of the book: There's a better way to pay for necessary services—one that doesn't strip people of real property ownership, force payment on unrealized gains, and let tax bills climb 50% or more in a few short years with no end in sight.

If we could develop a better way—shouldn't we?

That's the question this book is really asking.

The Beginning of the End of Property Taxes

In March of 2025, on the opening day of Florida's legislative session, I held a press conference. You can still watch it on my YouTube channel @RepRyanChamberlin.

The key line was this:

"We are at the beginning of the end of property taxes in the state of Florida."

I then filed a series of bills designed to create immediate relief, slow down the exponential growth of the system, and begin the longer conversation about a full transition away from a tax structure that has been operational in this state for almost 200 years—the system that made us life renters of our own property.

That press conference set off a frenzy of radio interviews, news articles, op-eds, and visits from city and county officials all wanting an answer to one question:

How are we going to replace the funding?

I quickly learned something important. The idea of eliminating property taxes can be a bipartisan concept. After all, no matter your political party, you're being crushed by the government when it comes to this out-of-control system. Republicans, Democrats, independents—the bill comes in the same envelope.

But the question of how to replace the revenue—that one is partisan. And that is where the real arguments tend to live.

- How do we pay for fire and police protection?
- How do we fund our schools?
- Who decides what constitutes a "necessary" expense currently funded by property taxes?

Those questions sit at the root of every property tax debate I've ever had in Tallahassee or at home in Marion County.

> *"There's a better way to pay for necessary services—one that doesn't strip people of real property ownership, force payment on unrealized gains, and let tax bills climb 50% or more in a few short years with no end in sight."*

After that press conference, I began a statewide conversation. Commissioners. Property appraisers. Sheriffs. Political clubs. School board members. Pastors. Concerned constituents. Realtors. Small business owners. Hundreds and hundreds of interactions.

I came away from those conversations with a clear conclusion. Most people don't like property taxes—but they can't wrap their heads around how local governments would pay for things.

And there lies a big problem. Because if we can't picture an alternative, we'll defend the system that's hurting us.

FREEDOM 1-2-3

It became clear by the summer of 2025 that nobody had a real plan they were willing to release—and nobody was willing to publicly debate one either. Not a politician. Not an association. Not a think tank.

So I decided it was time.

I was after the elimination of the entire system. But I also knew that to eliminate property taxes, we had to come to the table with a replacement strategy. Without that, we lose the debate before it starts.

In September of 2025, I held a second press conference (go to my YouTube Channel @RepRyanChamberlin to watch the pinned video). This time I was releasing a full plan. I called it Freedom 1-2-3.

This was the first full elimination and replacement plan filed in Florida in decades. And yes, it stirred things up. I knew the plan would be put through the ringer. As it should be.

But you can't debate a plan that doesn't exist. So I gave them one to debate. And here it is.

Freedom 1—The Rollback (Immediate Relief)

In Florida, property taxes are baked into the state constitution. What that means is the Legislature can't just pass a bill and eliminate them. It would take a legislative or citizen led constitutional amendment, which means a statewide ballot, which means 60% voter approval. That's a big reason it has been so hard to dismantle this system for as long as it has existed.

But there is a tool the Legislature can use right now: a rollback.

A rollback is a legislative mechanism where a bill is filed to revert the property tax collection rate and formula to a specific prior year. It has been done before.

It is designed for exactly the kind of situation we are in—when something gets out of control, the Legislature can press pause, revert to a previous year, and give itself the runway to work things out.

And what is our situation in Florida? Property taxes have risen by over 50% in just the last four years. Some counties saw increases of 82% or more. The local governments were never expecting this kind of windfall—but once they got it, they spent it, and built it into their baseline. A perfect storm was created that put an emergency level of pressure on every property owner in this state.

"Property taxes in Florida have risen by over 50% in just four years."

So in 2025, I filed a bill to roll property tax collections back to 2023 numbers—to give Florida citizens instant relief while we continued the longer fight for full elimination and replacement.

That bill cut roughly $12 billion in property taxes immediately.

"Freedom 1 delivers approximately $12 BILLION in immediate property tax relief to Floridians."

And of course, it was challenged. Loudly. By exactly the people whose job it is to spend that money. But here's what mattered: a bill was filed. A specific number was on the table. Hundreds of conversations followed. You can't debate a bill that doesn't exist.

Freedom 2—Removing Property Taxes from the Constitution

With Freedom 1 creating immediate relief, the next bill I filed was an HJR—a House Joint Resolution—to amend the Florida Constitution.

The amendment language was simple and surgical. Right now, Article VII, Section 1(a) of the Florida Constitution says no state ad valorem taxes shall be levied on real estate or tangible personal property. My amendment would change one line so that no ad valorem taxes of any kind shall be levied by any state, county, district, or municipal government entity upon real estate or tangible personal property.

In plain English: no government in Florida—state, county, city, or special district—would be allowed to place a lien on your property and collect taxes against it.

> *"This is the bill that makes elimination permanent."*

This is the necessary piece if we ever truly want to abolish property taxes. This is the once-and-for-all. Without this amendment, every fight is temporary. Every rollback can be undone. Every relief measure can be eroded over the next budget cycle. The constitutional ban is what makes the elimination permanent. Freedom

2 is the legal mechanism that makes "you actually own it" mean something.

I said this at my press conference, "Let me tell you what will happen before this amendment is approved. There will be panic. And let me tell you what will happen after the voters of Florida approve it. There will also be panic. But for the first time, it will be the government panicking about how to fund itself—instead of homeowners and small business owners panicking over how to pay their tax bill."

That, my friends, is a panic I am willing to live with.

Freedom 3—The Revenue Replacement Strategy

The final bill in the Freedom 1-2-3 plan was the first of its kind to address the elephant in the room—the question that had stopped every prior reform effort cold.

How are we going to pay for everything?

I will not pretend this question is small. It isn't. The state of Florida has roads to maintain. Sheriffs to fund. Firehouses to staff. Schools to run. Water management districts to operate. Nobody is interested in defunding the things that make our communities work. The conversation isn't whether we fund them. The conversation is how.

This is the right question. It is, in fact, the question. And for too long, it has been left unanswered—which is exactly why the conversation about eliminating property taxes has stalled for decades.

Freedom 3 is my answer.

I filed Freedom 3, legislation that, for the first time, put a real replacement framework on the table. A combination of transaction-based revenue, traveler-funded public safety contributions, and a dedicated school funding mechanism—designed to shift much of the burden onto the 143 million travelers who come to Florida every year and benefit from our police, our fire departments, and our public safety without contributing a dime through the property tax system.

> *"Today, 143 million travelers come to Florida every year and benefit from our police, our fire departments, and our public safety without contributing a dime through the property tax system."*

I'm not going to fully unpack the replacement numbers here. Part Three of this book is dedicated entirely to that conversation—the math, the mechanics, the assumptions, and the objections we've heard along the way. You deserve a thorough walk-through, and that's what I'll give you.

But here is the headline I want you to carry forward:

Florida has a $1.8 trillion economy. There is more than one way to fund the necessary services of the government. The property tax system is not the only option—it is just the only option anyone has been willing to defend.

Where This Leaves Us

Let me bring this back to where we started.

In the May 2026 special session, Governor DeSantis made history. HJR 1 took dead aim at the $18 billion in homestead property taxes and put Florida on a path to dramatically reduce—and in many cases eventually eliminate—the lien on our primary homes.

That is a historic step. We should celebrate it.

But Freedom 1-2-3 picks up where HJR 1 leaves off. Freedom 1-2-3 is the plan to continue what is now in motion—to eventually eliminate and replace the entire property tax system, on every parcel, for every owner.

Not because it's easy. Because it's right.

What I am proposing is not politically safe. There are powerful interests invested in the current system. There are institutions built around the assumption that property taxes are permanent. There are elected officials at every level of government who would rather have a quiet conversation about "reform" than a loud one about elimination.

But the people of Florida are not looking for quiet. They are looking for someone willing to say what they've been thinking for years.

This system is broken. It is fundamentally unjust. And we deserve something better.

That is what Freedom 1-2-3 says. Out loud. On the record. With a plan attached.

Part Three of this book will tell you exactly what that plan looks like—and why the future of property ownership in Florida doesn't have to look anything like the past.

The beginning of the end is already here.

What comes next is up to us.

Florida is already the freest state in the country. We have already been named the top state economy in the nation. If we do this—if we abolish the property tax once and for all and replace it with a system that does not turn citizens into renters of their own land—no one is going to be able to touch us.

We will be the first state in the country where you can actually own your own home.

We will be the first state in the country to say: we are not afraid of what is hard, only of what is wrong.

Part Three of this book will explain how.

Part Two

Key Takeaways

This fight is bigger than homestead exemption—the majority of non-homestead property taxes still burdens small businesses, farmers, and other owners.

Eliminating property taxes is bipartisan; replacing the revenue is not—that's where every real debate at the Capitol actually lives.

A legislative rollback delivers immediate relief—by reverting property tax collections to a previous year using an existing legislative mechanism.

A permanent fix requires a constitutional amendment—banning any Florida government entity from taxing or placing a lien on real estate, ever.

There is a better way to replace the revenue—for example, proposing transaction-based revenue and traveler-funded contributions from Florida's 143 million annual visitors instead.

You can't debate a plan that doesn't exist—Freedom 1-2-3 was filed so critics could finally have something concrete to argue against.

The goal remains full elimination and replacement—on every parcel, for every owner—not incremental reform.

Stay connected.
Scan for updates and to follow the movement.

EndPropertyTaxNow.com

"Now what liberty can there be, where property is taken away without consent?"

—Samuel Adams, "The Rights of the Colonists" (1772)

Part Three

A Better Way to Pay

With cameras rolling and reporters gripping their notepads, I closed my first property tax press conference with:

"I'll be happy to take any questions."

I'd anticipated the question that came next. But there's something different about standing at a podium, on the record, with mainstream news pointing a lens at you and asking the one question the establishment has been hiding behind for 30 years:

"Representative Chamberlin—how do you plan to pay for police, fire, and safety? Where will the money come from?"

That was a defining moment for me. Not because the question caught me off guard—it didn't. But because it was demonstrative of where this debate begins and ends for most people. They don't start by asking whether the system is fair. They start by asking who pays for it.

The rest of this chapter is rooted in one simple idea.

Anyone who tells you it's not possible to eliminate the current property tax system and replace what needs to be paid for is not telling you the truth.

"I'm talking about full elimination of property taxes on every property for every Floridian—for good—and it's entirely possible."

I'm not talking about a carve-out. I'm not talking about a homestead exemption that gets eaten by next year's millage rate hike. I'm talking about the entire system—for all properties. Homestead and commercial. Residential and agricultural. Every last lien-backed dollar the government currently extracts from the people who thought they owned their land.

Every property. Every Floridian. For good.

I want to be crystal clear about that, because one of the oldest political tricks in the book is to frame any ambitious reform as being "for some properties" or "only for certain homeowners." I am talking about full elimination. And it is completely achievable.

Two Kinds of Thinkers

After several years inside this conversation—in committee rooms, in town halls, on radio shows, across kitchen tables—I've come to a conclusion. When the stakes are this big, there are two kinds of thinkers in the room.

There are people who immediately ask, "How could we make that work?"

And there are people who immediately say, "That will never work."

Henry Ford said it best: "Whether you think you can, or you think you can't—you're right."

Florida has a $1.8 trillion economy. We are the 16th largest economy on planet Earth. We outproduce most countries. Only one state has a larger economy, and few states are growing faster.

And someone wants to look me in the eye and tell me we can't figure out a smarter way to fund police, fire, and schools than putting a permanent lien on every homestead in the state?

Come on.

Here's what's really going on. The current system has become a money grab—for so many people, in so many departments, with so many quietly embedded line items—that a full reset feels too disruptive to the very people who'd have to vote for it. The folks closest to the money have the most to lose if we audit it. So they don't want to audit it. They want to tell you it can't be done.

It's the easy answer. "We can't. Schools would suffer. Public safety would suffer." Fear is lazy; solutions require work.

In all my years laying the groundwork for this fight, I can count on one hand the number of county elected officials who've actually wanted to sit down and brainstorm replacement revenue with me. Most of them just want to circle the wagons and chant the line: "It can't be done."

It can be done. And in this chapter, I'm going to start proving it.

Freedom 3: The Solution Bill

When I filed what I call Freedom 3, it was entirely about solutions—opening the conversation about how we replace the revenue that property taxes currently generate.

But here's something critical to understand: Freedom 2 and Freedom 3 were designed to work together, and neither one works without the other.

Freedom 2 eliminates the government's ability to place a lien on your property for non-payment of taxes. That's the constitutional protection—the one that says you actually own your home. Freedom 3 is the revenue replacement mechanism. It's the proof that we've thought this through. That this isn't a slogan—it's a plan.

Which brings us to the question the gentleman from the mainstream news asked me at that press conference:

If we abolish property taxes for good—how do we replace the revenue?

What follows are four foundational ideas. These are not the only ideas—not by a long shot. They are the opening of a conversation that Florida desperately needs to have.

IDEA #1: Clean Up Fraud, Waste, and Misuse

I'm starting here, with Reason 4 from Part One of this book, because I believe this is the root cause of most of the resistance from counties and local leaders. To trim the budget and clean up fraud, you need accountability.

Accountability means questions. And questions like these make the establishment squirm:

- Why are tax dollars paying for this?
- Who authorized redirecting these funds to that department?
- Why did this line item triple over five years with no public vote?
- What's the ROI on this initiative—and who's measuring it?

Watch what happens at the next county commission meeting when somebody asks those out loud. You'll feel the tension immediately.

In Florida, between the second half of 2025 and the first half of 2026 alone, CFO Blaise Ingoglia has uncovered billions of dollars in fraud and waste through DOGE-style audits of local government. And he's just getting started.

Now layer that onto the conversation. Local officials are simultaneously telling you:

1. "We don't have enough money."
2. "There's no way we can cut property taxes."
3. "By the way, property tax collections are up 50% in just a few years."

And then a state CFO walks in and finds billions in fraud sitting right under the surface. It doesn't add up. And the people of Florida are catching on.

So let's do what any business owner would do when the books are bleeding—**trim the budget, cut the fraud**, and then see where we actually stand.

My personal belief—based on the numbers I've seen—is that if we rolled back property taxes to a reasonable baseline year and aggressively cut the fraud and waste, we could eliminate the roughly $18 billion in homestead property tax burden with that move alone. That's before we ever talk about a single new revenue stream.

IDEA #2: A Travel Safety Fee

Florida hosts 140 million visitors a year. One hundred and forty million.

When a tourist gets in a fender-bender on I-4. When a vacationer needs an ambulance at Disney. When a snowbird's rental car gets clipped on the Tamiami Trail. When somebody dials 911 from a short-term rental in Destin —

Who pays for the response? You do. The homeowner. Through your property tax bill.

Right now, Florida property owners are subsidizing the public safety services of 140 million people who don't live here. That is not a partisan statement. That is arithmetic.

A modest Travel Safety Fee—applied to airline tickets, rideshare trips, short-term vacation rentals, and amusement park admissions—would generate billions annually. It would shift a chunk of the property tax burden off the backs of Florida citizens and onto the tens of millions of travelers who are currently using our services for free.

This is just fair. If you fly into MCO, jump in an Uber, and stay at a beach rental for a week, you are using our roads, our deputies, our paramedics, and our fire response. A few dollars on the front end is a small price for the safety net you're benefiting from.

IDEA #3: A One-Time Property Sales Tax

Here's something most Floridians don't realize. There is no sales tax on real estate transactions in Florida. None.

You pay sales tax on a $30 pair of shoes. You pay sales tax on a $50,000 truck. But you can buy a $5 million property and pay essentially zero sales tax. Just a small documentary stamp.

What happens instead? You buy the property with no sales tax—and then you pay $3,000, $5,000, $10,000 a year, every year, forever. Stop paying and the government liens your property with the balance. That's not ownership. That's a rental.

In 2025, Florida had over $240 billion in property transactions.

Run the math on this example. A 5% one-time sales tax on real estate transactions in 2025 would have generated $12 billion in state revenue. In one year.

On a $300,000 home, that 5% tax would amount to a one-time payment of $15,000 at closing. The buyer can pay it, the seller can pay it, or the two parties can split it 50/50. We could even allow it to be financed over 36 months.

And once it's paid, you're done. No $5,000 annual bill for the rest of your life. No lien that follows your children and grandchildren.

You'd pay less over ten years than the current system costs you in three. And when it's over, you actually own the property.

IDEA #4: A Dedicated School Penny (or Two)

Now let me ask you a question that needs to be on the table.

Should everyone in Florida pay for our schools? Or should it just be the homeowners?

The school system is the single largest recipient of property tax revenue in this state. It's also the source of one of the most common frustrations I hear from Floridians, especially seniors, empty nesters, and homeowners with no children in the district, who are paying the largest line item on their tax bill for a service they don't directly use.

Here's the math the establishment doesn't want you to do: Every 1% of sales tax in Florida generates roughly $8 billion in annual revenue.

I'm not in love with sales tax. But let's compare the two options honestly:

Option A: Homeowners continue paying $3,000–$7,000 every year, forever, on a home they supposedly own—with the threat of losing it if they fall behind.

Option B: Add two pennies to the sales tax and spread the burden across everyone who participates in Florida's economy.

Just two cents—and every homestead property in the state of Florida pays zero in school tax ever again.

Why haven't we done this? I genuinely don't know.

When I pitch this to people, the pushback I hear most is: "Ryan, you're creating a new tax."

No. I'm not. You're already paying a school tax. It's just embedded as a lien on your home instead of spread across the broader economy.

I want to move it off your house and into the cash register—where every Floridian, every tourist, every visiting business contributes a fraction of a penny on each purchase to fund our kids' education.

And here's why. A 2% increase in sales tax costs you $20 for every $1,000 you spend on taxable purchases. Even if a household spent $50,000 a year on taxable goods, that would amount to roughly $1,000 in additional sales tax. For many homeowners, that's still far less than the school-related portion of their annual property tax bill.

This isn't just good for homeowners. Renters pay property taxes too—they just don't receive the bill. Those taxes are built into their rent and into the cost of housing across the state. By shifting this responsibility to a broader-based sales tax, we ask everyone who participates in Florida's economy—including the millions of tourists who use our roads, parks, and public services—to help fund those services. And any replacement should be designed to protect essential goods and avoid placing an unfair burden on lower-income families.

It's good math. It's fair math. And it's transparent—you can see it on every receipt instead of buried in a property assessment notice.

But even beyond the math the principle is better. A sales tax does not rise simply because your neighborhood became more valuable on paper. A sales tax does not create a lien on your home or threaten your ownership. Again, I am not saying this is the only answer. I am saying it is one serious answer that deserves to be part of the replacement conversation.

"You can't debate a plan that doesn't exist. This book is a plan."

First, we clean up fraud, waste, and misuse.

Second, we shift some of the burden created by tourism and travel onto the people using those services.

Third, we examine a one-time property transaction model instead of a lifetime annual property tax.

Fourth, we move school funding away from the property lien and into a broader, more transparent funding source.

I want to be direct: I believe that the four ideas above—properly developed, properly legislated, and properly implemented—could more than replace the $50+ billion in annual property tax revenue that currently funds Florida's government operations.

But I want to be equally direct about something else: these four ideas are the starting point. Not the finish line.

This Is Just the Beginning

We don't have to stop at just these four ideas. As we go further down this road more ideas and solutions will unfold. Ideas #5 through #10—and there will be many more—are the ones that emerge from what I call a well-organized discussion.

That's not a euphemism for endless committee meetings. It's a commitment to building a real, participatory process where Floridians help design the system that governs their property and their futures.

The truth is, we've never had this conversation in a serious way. Every time the discussion gets close to property tax replacement, we're told the sky will fall, the schools will close, or the roads won't get paved. The conversation gets shut down before it can begin. That has to change.

If we're going to replace a system this large, the process shouldn't be driven by fear. It should be driven by open debate, honest math, and the people who will have to live with the outcome.

Sure we can debate...

... how to generate revenue from non-Florida-based corporations that pull billions out of our economy while their headquarters are in Delaware or California.

... a fairer onboarding contribution from the new residents moving to Florida every single day—people who chose Florida specifically because of the opportunity it offers and who can help fund the infrastructure they just moved into.

... hard caps on local government spending growth so that even when the new system goes live, counties can't quietly inflate the budget back to where it was within five years.

... a percentage cap on millage equivalents so no future legislature, no future county commission, and no future school board can ever rebuild the tax-lien machine we just tore down.

... sin tax shifts, tourism surcharges, port-of-entry fees, large-event surcharges, and a dozen other revenue streams that put the burden where the usage actually is.

The key word in every one of those sentences is DEBATE.

These are just a handful of the conversations that belong on the table—and that I'll be pushing into the open in Part Four.

The future of Florida's tax system should be shaped by an open discussion of the best available options—not by the assumption that the current system is the only one that can work.

The current system works very well for government. It just doesn't work very well for the people paying the bill. And as I said earlier in this book—

You can't debate a plan that doesn't exist.

That's why this book exists. That's why FREEDOM 1, FREEDOM 2, and FREEDOM 3 exist. To put a real plan on the table so Florida can finally have the real debate.

I genuinely like the four ideas I presented above. I think they're a strong opening. But more important than any single one of them is the point they make:

If we want to figure out how to replace every dollar of property tax revenue in this state—we can.

And if we fully develop these ideas, alongside ideas #5 through #10 that will come from Floridians, business owners, sheriffs, school superintendents, economists, and yes—even the county commissioners who currently say it can't be done—we can build a new system that:

- Costs Floridians less,
- Is more fair and more transparent than the one we have,
- Stops punishing seniors and homesteaders disproportionately,
- And makes Florida the first state in the United States where you actually OWN your property.

That's not a slogan. It's a standard worth pursuing.

Asking the Right Questions: Root vs. Revenue

Since I started publicly carrying the flag for property tax elimination, I get questions every single day. Some are honest. Some are gotchas. Some come from policy folks who genuinely want solutions. Some come from people who are paid to make sure these reforms never happen.

I've noticed that almost every objection I get starts from one of two completely different places. I call them Root Thinking and Revenue Thinking.

Revenue Thinking starts at the cash register and asks: "How do we keep collecting what we currently collect?"

Root Thinking starts at the founding principle and asks: "Should the government ever have been collecting it this way in the first place?"

Let me show you what I mean.

Example #1

Revenue Thinking question: "Why would you want to eliminate property taxes on businesses? That's a huge revenue source."

Root Thinking answer: My objection isn't to the amount. My objection is to the mechanism. I believe it is a principle violation for the government to hold a permanent lien on your property—whether your home or your business. A small business owner who's spent 30 years building a deli, a tire shop, a daycare, or a family farm shouldn't have to keep paying the government rent on their own building forever just to keep operating. There is a better, fairer way to fund government than to permanently leverage every entrepreneur's life work.

The Revenue Thinker is asking: "How will we replace the money?" That's a legitimate technical question, and I just answered it with four ideas to open the conversation.

The Root Thinker is asking: "Why are we doing it this way in the first place?" That's the more important question—and it's the one this book is built on.

Example #2

Revenue question: "Property tax is one of the most stable revenue sources we have. What do we do in a recession?"

Root answer: Is it fair that every business, every household, and every retiree in Florida has to tighten their belt in a recession—but state and local governments don't have to? Is it fair that the citizens absorb every up and down of the economy while the government's revenue line goes up no matter what?

Here's how I'd answer the recession question concretely: the new model we build should be stress-tested against the highs and lows of the last 20–30 years in Florida. We model it against the 2008 collapse. We model it against COVID. We model it against the 2020s inflation spike. We model it against hurricane years. And then we build a budget that can handle the peak and the trough.

Part of how we got here is that for decades Florida was spending every dollar it took in—and then asking for more. That's changed. We've built a real reserve. We've got the cushion to weather a transition the smart way.

Bottom line: we should never keep collecting revenue through an unfair, principle-violating system just because it's politically convenient.

The Revenue Thinker sees a difficult problem and concludes it can't be done. The Root Thinker asks a different question: If the current system violates a fundamental principle, how do we replace it? Once we decide that preserving an unjust system is no longer an acceptable option, the conversation changes. The challenge is no longer whether it can be done, but how to do it wisely.

And if there is ever a true financial emergency—well, we do exactly what we've always done. Call a special legislative session. Bring Floridians the facts. And come up with a solution. That's how a free state is supposed to operate. Not by quietly leveraging your homestead in perpetuity.

Where We Go From Here

There is a long, detailed, technical, sometimes uncomfortable discussion ahead of us. There are real numbers to crunch and real models to build.

I'm ready. So is a growing army of Floridians.

To make sure every Floridian has a way to follow along, contribute ideas, weigh in on the trade-offs, and watch this fight unfold in real time—I've built a home for the movement at **EndPropertyTaxNow.com**.

That's where:

- The plan keeps evolving in public,
- Ideas #5 through #10 get crowdsourced from Floridians like you,
- The data and the models live out in the open,
- And the next round of action gets organized—district by district, county by county.

We're going on this journey together. The goal is simple to state and will be historic to accomplish:

Eliminate property taxes. Replace the revenue. Restore real ownership to every Floridian.

But how we get there matters as much as getting there. We will do it in a way that creates transparency, fairness, and what most Floridians would call common sense. No backroom deals. No hidden carve-outs. No swapping one form of bondage for another.

In Part Four, I'm going to show you exactly how we win this fight—how we rally Florida, county by county, to make this the law of the land once and for all. The strategy. The coalition. The pressure points. The timeline. The role you play.

This was the what and the why.

Part Four is the how.

Part Three

Key Takeaways

Full elimination is the goal—every property, every Floridian, for good—not a homestead-only carve-out that erodes with the next millage hike.

Fraud and waste cleanup alone could cover most of the homestead burden—audits have already found billions in improper spending, before any new revenue source is even added.

A Travel Safety Fee shifts costs onto visitors, not homeowners—Florida's 140 million annual tourists use police, fire, and EMS that homeowners currently fund alone through property taxes.

A one-time property sales tax replaces the lifetime bill—a financeable ~5% transaction tax means you pay once and actually finish paying—no annual bill forever.

A 1–2 cent sales tax could zero out school property taxes—shifting the largest line item on the tax bill off homesteads and onto everyone who spends money in Florida.

The plan is designed to be public and evolving—more ideas will be crowdsourced at EndPropertyTaxNow.com, setting up Part Four's playbook for actually winning the fight.

Join the conversation.
Scan to explore and share your ideas.

EndPropertyTaxNow.com

Part Four

The People's Amendment

"It's going to take a movement—and that's a big reason why I'm writing this book."

On April 1, 2026, I stood at the podium in the rotunda of the Florida capitol for my third property tax press conference. It wasn't a stunt, and it wasn't a victory lap. It was a turning point—the moment I stopped asking the legislature in Tallahassee for permission and started to talk about the idea of asking the people of Florida for their signature. You can watch the full press conference on my YouTube channel @RepRyanChamberlin. But before you do, let me tell you what that moment was really about, because it's the same thing this entire final part of the book is about.

Here is the truth I had to come to terms with, and the truth I need you to come to terms with too: it is highly unlikely that Florida's House, Senate, and Governor will ever fully agree to eliminate property taxes through the legislative process alone. The incentives in that building don't point toward giving up a guaranteed revenue stream. I've sat in those rooms. I've carried the bills. I know how hard that path is.

But there is another way.

And this other way doesn't depend on 160 legislators and one governor finding consensus. It depends on you. It depends on us, the people. It is a path that, once set in motion, the politicians cannot stop, slow-walk, or quietly kill in committee. That path is a citizen-led constitutional amendment—and on April 1st, I announced that I would begin to pursue this path.

A Path the People Own

Citizen-led constitutional amendments have changed Florida before. In recent years, voters used this exact process to put marijuana legalization and abortion rights directly on the ballot—bypassing a legislature that wouldn't act on its own.

What has never happened, not once in the history of the United States, is a citizen-led property tax ballot initiative passing to create true home ownership.

We're about to make history.

But realize—that when we get this on the ballot, and when it is voted on. It's still not over.

Then and only then will the legislature be forced to **implement** NEW solutions to make sure we have a new system in place for funding the POLICE, FIRE DEPARTMENTS, and SCHOOLS.

How It Works

Property taxes are written into Florida's constitution. That means any fundamental change to them has to be voted on by the entire population of the state—not just a handful of committee chairs. Once the question reaches the ballot, it needs 60% approval to pass.

There are exactly two ways to get a constitutional question in front of voters.

Path 1: The Legislative Route. The House and Senate agree, the Governor signs off, and the question goes to the ballot. This is the path I've been fighting for inside the building—and as Part Two laid out, it's an uphill climb.

Path 2: The Citizen Route. It's the signature path. The people write the language, get it approved, and gather signatures from registered voters across the state. When the threshold is hit, it goes on the ballot *with or without the permission of the House, the Senate, or the Governor.*

That second path is the one we just opened. **It will be up to the people. It will be up to you.**

> *"There is a constitutional path to freedom that depends on us, the people—one that politicians cannot stop."*

As of this writing, the citizen-initiative requirements in Florida are:

- Properly drafted and approved constitutional language, plus
- 880,062 verified signatures from registered voters.

Hit those two milestones, and the question goes on the ballot.

If it passes with 60% of the vote, three things happen—automatically—by force of constitutional law:

1. The government's ability to place a lien on your property is permanently eliminated.
2. The legislature is constitutionally required to implement a replacement revenue plan.
3. Florida becomes the first state in the United States where you genuinely own your property.

This is also exactly why having the replacement conversation now, before the vote, is so important. That's what Freedom 1-2-3 and the revenue replacement strategy in Part Three are built for. The smartest path forward is to have the conversation—and the consensus—on replacement revenue before the ballot vote. So that when Floridians cast their vote, they're voting for a path forward, not into uncertainty. We're not asking Florida to leap blind. We're building the landing pad first.

Could This Really Work?

If you've made it this far in the book, I already know something about you. You're tired of renting property you supposedly own. You're tired of paying taxes on gains you haven't even realized. You know a 50% increase in your tax bill over a few years isn't a coincidence—it's a system working exactly as designed, just not in your favor. And you've seen enough waste and fraud in how those dollars get spent to know the problem isn't a lack of revenue. It's a lack of accountability.

You probably don't have a lot of faith that the government is going to fix this on its own. So you're asking the only honest question left:

Could something like this actually work?

Let's Lay It Out, Honestly

I'm not going to sell you a fantasy. Here's the truth, plain and simple:

- This will require resolve.
- This will require organization.
- This will require education.
- This will require resources.

But here's what gives me confidence: the state itself built this rule for a reason. The framers of Florida's constitutional amendment process understood that sometimes the people need a way around a legislature that won't move. That rule exists so that if enough people want something badly enough—they can get it done. The founders of our state constitution built this lane on purpose, for moments exactly like this one. No permission required. No committee chair to convince. Just signatures, and the will to gather them.

What If It Doesn't Work?

Here's the thought I want you to sit with for a minute—the one I sat with for months before I decided to go all in: What if we do all of this, and it doesn't pass?

Here's my honest answer: you're no worse off than you are today. Your tax bill doesn't go up because we tried.

In fact, I'd argue you're better off. Substantially better off. Why?

Because the sheer effort of an organized, statewide signature drive becomes impossible for any elected official to ignore. Hundreds of thousands of Floridians showing up, signing their names, and demanding change sends a signal that no press release or committee hearing ever could.

Every county commissioner, state representative, state senator, candidate for governor, candidate for CFO, superintendent, and sheriff—every single one of them will know that a movement of this size exists, that it is organized, that it is funded, that it is voting, and that it is not going away.

> *"The framers of Florida's constitutional amendment process understood that sometimes the people need a way around a legislature that won't move."*

At some point, that kind of pressure forces correction in the system—whether it happens through this amendment or through the legislature finally getting serious about the replacement plan. Either way, you win. The only way you lose is by sitting this one out.

How Do We Get to 880,062?

This is a large number of petitions, and there are going to be many special interests and entrenched local elected officials who will fight our trying to collect these petitions because they do not want the status quo to change. But if we stand up and work together, we can get it done.

Here's the plan, and here's exactly where you fit into it.

1. Sign the Petition

Your signature matters. Once you sign, drive everyone you know who would have interest to **EndPropertyTaxNow.com/petition** to download, sign the petition, and physically mail it—yes mail it.

2. Spread the Word

Share this book with your neighbor. We've made it easy to sponsor and buy 10, 100, 1,000 copies at a highly discounted price!

Every copy is a door opener, a conversation starter, and a potential signature.

A book sitting in a warehouse changes nothing. A book in the hands of a fed-up Florida homeowner changes everything.

When you sponsor, we make distribution easy. You pick the path that fits you:

- **Option A: Ship them to you.** You hand them out personally. Church. Small business. HOA meeting. PTA. The folks in your circle who trust your voice more than any politician's.
- **Option B: Our team distributes.** We have boots on the ground in every Florida county. You sponsor, we deploy.
- **Option C: Secure a sponsor and host an event.** You can invite me to come speak to your organization, on a podcast, or for a Zoom.

Every book you put in someone's hand is a soldier added to this movement. Multiply the message and watch what happens.

Order your books at
EndPropertyTaxNow.com/book

3. Fuel the Movement

This book does double duty. It educates the masses and generates ballot signatures, and it helps fund the movement itself— which means we don't need to rely on the kind of massive donor funding most ballot initiatives require. The book pays its own way forward.

Remember the number: 880,062 signatures. If we build an army of Floridians who are organically sharing this message—at the dinner table, at church, at the office, on social media—this can happen faster than anyone in Tallahassee expects.

And it all begins with your signature.

Profits from this book go directly to:

- Training and deploying signature gatherers
- Funding the legal team that defends the ballot language
- Producing graphics, ads, and digital content for the grassroots army
- Powering the technology platform at **EndPropertyTaxNow.com**
- Funding End Property Tax Now speaking engagements

This is how we **fund the movement without becoming dependent on big-money donors** the way most ballot initiatives have to. The book is the fundraiser, the message, and the membership card.

We also welcome volunteers to help us pass out books at events, and go door-to-door collecting signatures. Stay involved as the movement grows.

EndPropertyTaxNow.com/volunteer

LET'S DO THIS TOGETHER

Every movement in this country has started the same way—with a small number of people who decide, "I'm in."

They had conviction. And the movement followed.

Go to **EndPropertyTaxNow.com** right now and do the following:

- **Sign the petition.** Yours is signature #1 in your household. Get the rest of your family on next.

- **Sign up for movement updates** so you don't miss a single milestone, rally, or county-by-county push.
- **Sponsor books**—10, 100, 1,000—at whatever level fits you. Every copy is one more Floridian in the fight.
- **Plan an event at** your church, your business, your county GOP, your Rotary club, your HOA. If you've got a room of Floridians who care, I'll fill it.
- **Join our LIVE Zoom updates** (free, occasional)—real-time strategy, numbers, and wins, straight from me to you.
- **Become a volunteer** to pass out books or help support events where I speak on this topic.
- **Download the free graphics and share them** across social media—Facebook, X, Instagram, TikTok, your church group chat, your business newsletter.

Property taxes have never been eliminated by a citizen-led amendment, anywhere in this country, in the entire history of the United States. Florida is going to be the state that proves it can be done. Not because Tallahassee decided to give us this right—but because we took it, signature by signature, exactly the way the constitution allows.

You don't have to wait for permission. You don't have to wait for the next legislative session. You don't have to wait for someone else to go first.

Your signature. That is where this begins. Not with a politician. Not with a committee. Not with a lobbyist. Not with a special interest. With you.

Your signature says:

I want this question on the ballot.

I believe the people of Florida should decide.

I am ready to have the conversation.

Your signature does not require every detail to be perfect today. It requires believing that the current system is broken enough that the people deserve a vote.

EndPropertyTaxNow.com

A Final Word—From One Floridian to Another

I didn't run for office to be a politician. I ran because I believe Florida is the freest, boldest, most opportunity-rich state in the union—and we still aren't even close to the freedom we were created to enjoy. Property tax elimination is one of the last great fights left between true ownership and permanent rental of our own land.

> *"I envision Florida as the freest state in the union—the first one where you will actually own your property."*

Florida has led before. We have led on freedom, growth, and opportunity. We have led on school choice, economic strength, entrepreneurship, tourism, and migration. People move to Florida because they believe something is different here. They believe Florida still represents possibility. They believe Florida is a place where families can build, businesses can grow, and freedom still matters.

Now Florida has a chance to lead again. We can become the first state in America to say:

If you paid for your property, you should own your property.

And if Florida does it, other states will follow.

That is how big this is. This is not just about your next tax bill. This is about whether the next generation will inherit a system of ownership or a system of permanent taxation.

It is about whether young families will still believe they can buy a home and build a future. It is about whether retirees can stay in the homes they worked their whole lives to pay for. It is about whether business owners can build without being punished every year for owning their property. It is about whether property rights still mean something in America.

I cannot do this alone. No representative can. No senator can. No governor can.

But ***we*** can.

We can be the generation of Floridians that finally hands our children a state where the deed in the courthouse actually means what it says. Where "I own my home" is a complete sentence—not a sentence followed by "as long as I keep paying the government."

We can be the people who, 50 years from now, get pointed to in the history books with a single line: "That's the generation that made Florida the first free state in the union—where you actually own your property."

Part Four

Key Takeaways

A citizen-led constitutional amendment puts the people in charge—the first citizen-led effort in U.S. history to eliminate property taxes.

In Florida, it requires two milestones—approved ballot language plus 880,062 verified voter signatures, then 60% voter approval on election day.

Passing it triggers three automatic outcomes—the government's lien power ends, the legislature must implement a replacement plan, and Florida becomes the first state with true property ownership.

Even failure leaves Floridians no worse off—and the scale of an organized signature drive alone pressures officials to act, win or lose.

The plan runs on three steps—sign the petition, spread the word by sponsoring and distributing the book, and fuel the movement with the proceeds or donations.

This book funds the movement directly—training signature gatherers, legal defense of the ballot language, grassroots content, and the EndPropertyTaxNow.com platform—without relying on big donors.

The stakes are generational—this is framed as the fight to make "I own my home" a complete sentence in Florida for the first time, and a model other states could follow.

Take the next step.
Scan to sign the petition, get updates, and learn how to help.

EndPropertyTaxNow.com

JOIN THE MOVEMENT

★ ★ ★

The conversation starts with this book.
The movement starts with you.

Whether you're ready to take action today or simply stay informed, everything starts with one scan.

EndPropertyTaxNow.com

Scan to join the movement and:

- Sign the Petition
- Stay Updated
- Volunteer
- Sponsor More Books

★ ★ ★

Together, we can make Florida the first state where **ownership means ownership.**

Press Coverage

Major News Coverage of The Property Tax Reform Effort

Date	Article Title	Publication	Year
June 26, 2024	**Is Ryan Chamberlin's Property Tax Ploy Just a Service Tax in Disguise?**	*Florida Politics*	**2024**
March 5–6, 2025	**Rep. Ryan Chamberlin Pushes to End Property Taxes in Florida**	*Florida's Voice / FL Voice News*	**2025**
March 7, 2025	**Rep. Ryan Chamberlin Announces Plans to Eliminate Property Taxes in Florida**	*The Floridian*	**2025**
March 5–6, 2025	**Florida Senate Panel Wants Study on Property Tax Changes**	*WUSF Public Media / News Service of Florida*	**2025**
September 17, 2025	**Ryan Chamberlin Rolls Out Plan to Get Rid of Property Taxes**	*Florida Politics*	**2025**
February 19, 2026	**Florida House Passes Proposed Amendment to Immediately Phase Out Property Taxes**	*WLRN / Florida Phoenix*	**2026**
April 2, 2026	**Ryan Chamberlin Seeks Citizen Ballot Petition to Eliminate Property Taxes**	*The Floridian*	**2026**
April 9, 2026	**Ryan Chamberlin Proposes 2028 Property Tax Ballot Initiative**	*FlaglerLive*	**2026**
April 10, 2026	**Florida Lawmaker Champions Effort to Abolish Property Taxes**	*Florida Real Estate Wire*	**2026**
April 13, 2026	**Why Rep. Ryan Chamberlin Wants to Eliminate and Replace Florida's Property Taxes**	*WUSF / WLRN / WUWF (NPR Florida Network)*	**2026**

Upcoming Releases

Thank You For Your Service – Bringing Honor and Healing to All Veterans by Colonel Tim Cole and Representative Ryan Chamberlin

Veterans often downplay their service, leaving many family members and friends unaware of the sacrifices they have made. Colonel Tim Cole and Representative Ryan Chamberlin explore how recognizing that service can bring both the honor and healing our veterans deserve.

All In! –What Are You Willing to Go ALL IN on, with No Way Out? by Ryan Chamberlin

Drawing on more than 25 years of experience in leading organizational growth to more than 150,000 people along with his experience as a Florida legislator, Ryan Chamberlin shares a proven framework for messaging and building high-performance teams that embrace extraordinary commitment to one another and to a shared mission.

My Life as a Seminar Promoter: Lessons From Jim Rohn and Other Legends I Promoted by Kyle Wilson

Kyle Wilson shares lessons from 35 years producing events, publishing books, and working with personal development icons including Jim Rohn, Brian Tracy, Les Brown, Darren Hardy, and many others.

To learn more and pre-order, go to KyleWilson.com/books

Additional Resources

- **Watch press conferences** to learn more about the vision and progress of the movement.
- **Listen to podcasts** on property tax reform, leadership, and public policy.
- **Explore videos, articles, and educational resources** that explain the issues and proposed solutions.
- **Receive the latest** campaign news, updates, and volunteer opportunities.
- **Sign the petition** and help move the effort forward.

And more at EndPropertyTaxNow.com

Stay Connected with End Property Tax Now

IG: @endpropertytaxnow

FB: @endpropertytaxnow

X: @endproptaxnow

Stay Connected with Ryan Chamberlin

IG: @ryanchamberlin

FB: @repryanchamberlin

YT: @repryanchamberlin

X: @RepRyanC

RyanChamberlin.com • RepRyanChamberlin.com

Media Tour – End Property Tax Now

Bringing the Conversation to Communities Across Florida and Beyond

Ryan Chamberlin is committed to educating citizens, engaging community leaders, and advancing the conversation about ending property taxes through media appearances, public speaking, and educational events.

His work has been featured by **FOX News, TEDx, Newsmax,** SUCCESS, and **the Florida House of Representatives.**

Book Ryan on Your Podcast, Radio, or TV Show

Ryan has been featured in television interviews, podcasts, online publications, and speaking engagements discussing property tax reform, economic freedom, and citizen-led constitutional change.

Book Ryan to Speak

Ryan is available for:

- Podcasts
- Radio and television interviews
- Media tours

For speaking engagements and media inquiries, visit:
RyanChamberlin.com or EndPropertyTaxNow.com

Ryan Chamberlin

Author · Advisor · Advocate

Ryan Chamberlin came to politics the long way—

Twenty-five years as an entrepreneur and multiple-business owner before he ever ran for anything.

Starting from a kitchen table, he built and led a national business sustaining a large organization coast to coast, and spent decades teaching ordinary people how to build something of their own.

He is the author of five political, leadership, and entrepreneurial development books, a TEDx speaker, and the founder of **End Property Tax Now**.

In 2023, he was elected to the Florida House of Representatives for District 24, where he has become one of the loudest voices for returning true property ownership to the people who paid for it.

Today, alongside his work in the legislature, Ryan advises and speaks for founders, companies, conferences, and movements helping them define a message that spreads and a system that scales.

It's the same thing he's taught for three decades: nothing worthwhile happens alone, and the biggest results still start with one person deciding they're all in.

To connect with Ryan,
email **Contact@RyanChamberlin.com** or
fill out the form at **Connect.RyanChamberlin.com**.

Bring Ryan In

Founders, companies, conferences, and movements bring Ryan in to:

- **Speak** — keynotes, breakouts and podcast on freedom and entrepreneurship, building high performance teams, and why you don't own it until we end the property tax.
- **Advise** — a seat on the board, and/or strategy for founders, sales organizations, and advocacy movements that need a message that spreads and a system that scales.
- **Coach** — hands-on leadership and team development drawn from three decades in the trenches, not a textbook.

How to Engage with Ryan

As an advisor, Ryan specializes in:

- Business development consulting
- Board advisory for public and non-public companies
- Government relations and legislative affairs
- Strategic growth and performance

As an author and speaker, Ryan can support your organization through:

- Live keynotes and corporate events
- Zoom series and courses
- Leadership and high-performance team training (corporate and field)
- Podcast guest appearances

To connect with Ryan,
email **Contact@RyanChamberlin.com** or
fill out the form at **Connect.RyanChamberlin.com.**

About the Author

Ryan Chamberlin is a member of the Florida House of Representatives, where he fights to safeguard individual freedom, strengthen Florida's economy, and defend the conservative, faith-rooted values that families across the state count on. Since being sworn in in 2023, he has worked through legislation and advocacy to keep government limited, protect free enterprise, and put citizens ahead of bureaucracy.

That conviction was forged over a 25-year career building people and businesses. Ryan has helped thousands of entrepreneurs and business leaders build organizations that last. He is the author or co-author of several books on politics, entrepreneurship, leadership, and marketing, a TEDx speaker, and the founder of End Property Tax Now, a non-profit organization advocating for true property ownership free from government liens. He brings this same experience to companies as a strategic advisor and keynote speaker.

Ryan lives in Central Florida with Jenny, his wife of 32 years. Together they have four adult sons, four daughters-in-law, and one grandson.

Ryan Chamberlin
Author • Advocate • Advisor
Member, Florida House of Representatives

Buy in Bulk for Discounts and Bonuses

Level	Quantity	Price	Shipping
	1–9	$12.97 ea	Plus Shipping
Basic	10+	$10 ea	FREE SHIPPING plus Bonuses
Bronze	100+	$8.50 ea	FREE SHIPPING plus Bonuses
Silver	250+	$7.50 ea	FREE SHIPPING plus Bonuses
Gold	500+	$6 ea	FREE SHIPPING plus Bonuses
Platinum	1000+	$5 ea	FREE SHIPPING plus Bonuses

FREE SHIPPING for all orders of 10 or more books (US 48 states only)

Basic Sponsorship Bonuses (10+ Books)
Free Shipping plus recognition on EndPropertyTaxNow.com

Bronze Sponsorship Bonuses (100+ Books)
Free Shipping plus Bronze recognition on EndPropertyTaxNow.com
Limited Edition Hardback signed by Ryan Chamberlin
Special Edition Bronze *End Property Tax Now – Challenge Coin*

Silver Sponsorship Bonuses (250+ Books)
Free Shipping plus Silver recognition on EndPropertyTaxNow.com
Limited Edition Hardback signed by Ryan Chamberlin
Special Edition Silver *End Property Tax Now – Challenge Coin*
Ryan will appear for your group on Zoom or by podcast

Gold Sponsorship Bonuses (500+ Books)
Free Shipping plus Gold recognition on EndPropertyTaxNow.com
Two Limited Edition Hardbacks signed by Ryan Chamberlin
Two Special Edition Silver *End Property Tax Now – Challenge Coins*
Ryan will appear on Zoom, a podcast, or **live at your event**

Platinum Sponsorship Bonuses (1000+ Books)
Free Shipping plus Gold recognition on EndPropertyTaxNow.com
Five Limited Edition Hardbacks signed by Ryan Chamberlin
Five Special Edition Silver *End Property Tax Now – Challenge Coins*
Ryan will appear on Zoom, a podcast, or **live at your event**
Private lunch or dinner with Ryan before your event